# FOR THE FLOOR

## SEASON ONE | FOUNDATIONS



Amber Rae Lihs

For the Floor, Season One | Foundations

First Edition

By Amber Rae Lihs



Published by LTC Elevate, LLC

ISBN 979-8-218-92688-5

Cover design by Amber Rae Lihs using licensed elements.

Interior images created with licensed elements.

In honor of my grandma,
whose journey through aging and
long-term care gave direction to my
life and continues to shape the work
I do today.

# Contents

"Some of the most impactful parts of care often happen in the moments that don't make it into charts or job descriptions."

Hello there, I'm so glad you're here!

My journey into senior living began as a teenager, when my grandmother moved into long-term care. Like many families, we experienced a mix of emotions as she navigated a major life transition. Concern, hope, uncertainty, and grief. Watching her let go of independence, downsize a lifetime of belongings, and learn to accept help in new ways gave me an early window into the emotional side of aging.

Not long after, I began volunteering. What started as "helping out" quickly became something deeper. I became a nursing assistant, spending my days on the floor — assisting with care, listening to stories, noticing rhythms, and learning what it really means to show up for someone else. Over time, my role evolved into life enrichment and later into leadership, but the heart of the work never changed.

What stayed with me — and still does — is this: some of the most impactful parts of care often happen in the moments that don't make it into charts or job descriptions.

A shared laugh in the hallway.
A hand held a little longer than required.

A preference remembered.
A person truly seen.

Throughout my career, I've been drawn to the human side of care. The emotional, relational, and creative ways we support quality of life for older adults and for the teams who care for them. I believe deeply that connection is not an "extra" in this work; it is essential. And I believe that direct care teams already carry extraordinary wisdom, skill, and heart — they simply need space to reflect, share, and grow together.

This guide was created as a companion for that space.

Not as a training.
Not as a checklist.
But as an invitation to pause, to notice, and to remember why this work matters so much.

I'm grateful to walk alongside you,
Amber Rae

# How to Use This Guide

This guide is designed to be flexible and easy to use. Each chapter corresponds with an episode from Season One of the For the Floor podcast and can be used in department meetings, team gatherings, new employee orientation, or one-on-one conversations.

Each chapter follows a simple flow. You'll begin with a short description of the topic and a QR code to listen to the episode, followed by a featured quote to help ground your time together. Conversation prompts then offer space for reflection and discussion. Choose one question or explore several. There is no required order and no expectation to complete everything.

Each section also includes space for notes, whether that's capturing reflections, writing down kudos, or recording ideas you want to return to as a team.

You may choose to listen together or invite team members to listen ahead of time. Spend five minutes or fifty. Move in order or jump around. This guide is meant to support you without adding more to plan, prepare, or manage.

The purpose is not to resolve or summarize, but to encourage continued awareness and shared understanding, with each section ending in an invitation to carry these reflections back onto the floor and into everyday care.

# Season One | Foundations

Season One of For the Floor focuses on the foundations of care.

This season returns to the core of the work, the human experience at the heart of senior living. It invites teams to slow down, notice what matters, and reflect on how care is felt and lived each day, even in the midst of busy shifts and full responsibilities.

Across these episodes, we explore what shapes quality of life beyond tasks and outcomes, including presence, connection, and intention. Perspectives drawn from art, music, play, and shared experience help give teams a common language and a clearer understanding of how meaningful connection shows up in everyday care.

These conversations are not meant to provide answers or directives. They are designed to open dialogue, encourage reflection, and support leaders in strengthening their teams as these ideas carry back onto the floor.

Season One sets a shared starting point. It lays the groundwork for consistent, thoughtful care and helps teams move forward together with greater clarity, confidence, and purpose.

# Episode 1

## From the Beginning: Why For the Floor Matters

Before tasks, before titles, before roles — there is purpose. This episode invites you to reconnect with the heart behind the work and to remember why the human side of care matters so deeply, for residents and for ourselves.

We don't just meet biological care needs, we restore connection. And connection is just as vital as food, water, or medicine.

# Conversation Prompts

**1** — What originally drew you to this work, and what has kept you here?

**2** — When do you feel most connected to the why behind what you do?

**3** — In what moments do you notice that connection matters just as much as tasks or outcomes?

**4** — How do residents experience belonging through the people who work here?

**5** — What helps you reconnect to purpose on days that feel heavy or rushed?

# Notes

# An Invitation

As you return to your work, carry a quiet
reminder of why you chose this field.
Let that sense of purpose guide the
way you move through your shift.
Especially in the small moments that
may not be noticed, but matter
so much.

## The Human Side of Care: The Magic in the In-Between

Care is not only experienced in what we do, but in how we do it. This episode centers presence. The pauses, glances, breaths, and small moments that often carry the most meaning.

Care often lives in the pauses. In the moments we choose to slow down and truly see one another.

# Conversation Prompts

**1** — What are some small, in-between moments on your shift that tend to stay with you?

**2** — How does slowing down — even briefly — change the way an interaction feels?

**3** — What helps you reset when you feel rushed, overwhelmed, or distracted?

**4** — Where do you notice presence already showing up naturally in your work? Where could it be added?

**5** — How might one intentional pause change the tone of your day or someone else's?

# Notes

# An Invitation

As you head back onto the floor, allow
yourself to slow down just enough to
notice the moments in between tasks.
Even a brief pause, a breath, or a look
can change how care feels — for others
and for you.

# Episode 3

## Personhood: Seeing the Whole Human

Personhood lives beyond charts and routines. This episode invites a deeper kind of knowing. A knowing rooted in curiosity, meaning, and the understanding that dignity grows when people feel truly seen.

Facts tell us about someone. Essence helps us understand who they are.

# Conversation Prompts

1. When you think of a resident you know well, what comes to mind beyond their care needs?

2. How does knowing someone's story change the way you approach care?

3. What helps you move from knowing facts about someone to understanding their essence?

4. How does sharing meaningful details with teammates strengthen care across shifts?

5. What is one small way personhood could be honored more intentionally this week?

# Notes

# An Invitation

As you move through your next shift, hold the intention to see at least one person beyond what needs to be done. Let curiosity guide you toward who they are, not just what they need.

## Lessons from Okinawa: Elders as Treasure

How we see aging quietly shapes how we care. This episode offers a shift in perspective — from aging as decline to aging as accumulation, wisdom, and value.

Aging isn't about
what's lost, it's about
what's collected.

# Conversation Prompts

1. What messages about aging did you grow up with, and how do they still influence you?

2. How does seeing elders as "treasure" shift the way you think about care?

3. Where do you notice wisdom or resilience in the residents you serve?

4. How might celebrating age more openly change the environment in our community?

5. How do your beliefs about your own aging shape how you show up for others?

# Notes

# An Invitation

As you continue your work, carry with you the idea that aging holds value, wisdom, and beauty. Let that perspective quietly shape the way you speak, listen, and offer respect throughout your day.

## Lessons From Okinawa: Beyond Words

Not all communication is spoken. This episode explores the language of presence — body language, tone, energy, and rhythm. Especially when words are difficult or unavailable.

Long before words are

understood,

energy is felt.

# Conversation Prompts

1. Think of a time when connection happened without many words. What made it work?

2. How do posture, pace, and facial expression affect the way residents respond to you?

3. What does calm presence feel like in your body, and how do you access it?

4. How does energy shift in a room when someone enters grounded versus rushed?

5. What is one way you could let your presence speak more clearly this week?

# Notes

# An Invitation

As you step back into your work, be mindful of the energy you bring into each space. Your presence, posture, and pace often communicate care long before words ever do.

Belonging grows when people are included as participants, not observers. This episode explores how creativity and play dissolve barriers and bring people together as equals.

It's about what happens through them — the stories that surface, the memories that reappear, and the emotions that reconnect people who thought connection was lost.

# Conversation Prompts

**1** What makes you feel a sense of belonging — at work or elsewhere?

**2** How does creating with others feel different from doing something for them?

**3** Why do you think play and creativity are so powerful across ages and abilities?

**4** Where do you already see belonging being built in small, everyday ways?

**5** What is one creative invitation you could extend this week to help someone feel included?

# Notes

# An Invitation

As you move forward, look for small ways to invite others into shared experiences. Belonging is built when people feel included, valued, and free to participate in their own way.

## Inspiring Participation & Joy Through Art

Participation is an act of trust. This episode explores how gentle invitation, encouragement, and joy help people move from hesitation to connection.

It's not about being perfect, it's about being present.

# Conversation Prompts

1. Can you remember a time you were hesitant to participate but felt glad afterward?

2. How does a personal invitation feel different from a general announcement?

3. What does participation look like beyond actively "doing" an activity?

4. How does celebrating effort instead of outcome change the experience for people?

5. How does shared joy through laughter, creativity, and presence shape the way a day feels?

# Notes

# An Invitation

As you return to the floor, remember that participation grows through gentle invitation and encouragement. Creating space for joy and creativity can transform hesitation into connection — for residents and for teams.

## Bridging Rhythm with Joy and Connection

Caring deeply requires nourishment. This episode invites rhythm, joy, and simplicity back into the day as ways to sustain connection — for residents and caregivers alike.

"There are moments that don't require words. Moments where presence, rhythm, and shared energy carry more than language ever could."

# Conversation Prompts

**1.** What helps you feel regulated, grounded, or restored during your day?

**2.** How does music or rhythm show up naturally in your work already?

**3.** Where do you tend to overcomplicate things — and what might "keeping it simple" offer?

**4.** How does shared joy help you continue doing this work long-term?

**5.** What is one small, joyful moment you could intentionally create on your next shift?

# Notes

# An Invitation

As you continue this work, allow rhythm, music, and moments of joy to support you. Caring well for others becomes sustainable when we also make space to replenish ourselves along the way.

# Episode 9

## Language of Care

The words we use shape perception — and perception shapes care. This episode invites mindful awareness of language and its quiet power to honor or diminish personhood.

The way we speak
about our work shapes
how it is felt, by
others and
by ourselves.

# Conversation Prompts

⋅ ⋅ ◇ ⋅ ⋅

**1** What words or phrases do we use often that shape how we see residents or our work?

**2** How does person-first language change the way care feels — for you and others?

**3** How does the way we talk about our work influence how we feel about it?

**4** What is one word or phrase you might gently shift to be more human-centered?

**5** How might elevating our language help change the broader story of aging and care?

# Notes

# An Invitation

As you move forward, let your words reflect the dignity and humanity of the people you serve and the work you do. Small shifts in language can quietly shape culture, connection, and care over time.

# Podcast Host & Author Bio

Guided by a belief that aging is a season rich with purpose and possibility, Amber Rae Lihs uses photography and thoughtful reflection to honor personhood, celebrate life fully lived, and highlight the vital role direct care teams play in quality of life.

Serving residents directly on the floor shaped Amber's deep appreciation for both the work itself and the people who do it. That foundation continues to guide her leadership and her advocacy for aging services, including advocacy days at the Nebraska State Capitol and a congressional briefing on Capitol Hill in Washington, DC.

Today, Amber remains deeply dedicated to enhancing quality of life for aging adults. A recipient of the 2025 Champion of Innovation Award from the Nebraska Health Care Association, she holds certifications in gerontology, dementia, Montessori dementia, and support group facilitation, and is licensed as an Assisted Living Administrator. She founded the nonprofit Golden Gen Movement, coordinated the docuseries People Worth Caring About - Nebraska, and created For the Floor, a podcast and learning series designed to support leaders in supporting their teams, all with the shared goal of honoring aging adults and those who serve them.

# Acknowledgements

This work exists because of the many people who believe in the heart of care.

Thank you to everyone who has supported, celebrated, and shared their voice through the For the Floor podcast, and to those who show up each day for care teams in big and small ways. Whether through conversation, encouragement, leadership, or quiet presence, your contributions ripple far beyond what can be measured.

Most of all, thank you to the direct care teams who do this work with compassion, resilience, and heart. Your dedication is the foundation of everything this guide hopes to support.

Thank you to the family, friends, and colleagues who understand and support the vision I hold for uplifting care teams and providing the highest possible quality of life for those we serve. Giving me the space to dream, create, and bring this work to life means more than words can express.

www.ingramcontent.com/pod-product-compliance
Lightning Source LLC
Chambersburg PA
CBHW040915110726
48005CB00006B/896

This guide was created for those who lead from the floor.

For those who listen deeply, care fiercely, and understand that the human side of care is where quality of life is shaped.

For the Floor is a companion guide to the For the Floor podcast, created for senior living leaders and teams who value connection, reflection, and thoughtful care. Rooted in real experiences from the floor, it offers space for conversation that strengthens culture, collaboration, and the way care is experienced each day.

This guide is meant to support the moments between tasks. The ones that shape how care is felt, not just how it is delivered.